# IT LOOKS LIKE A C**K!

# IT LOOKS LIKE A C**K!

**BEN & JACK**

St. Martin's Griffin
New York

www.stmartins.com

Designed by the Members of Unreal, 20 Rugby Street, London WC1N 3QZ
www.unrealdesign.co.uk

Library of Congress Cataloging-in-Publication Data Available Upon Request

ISBN-13: 978-0-312-59503-6

First published in Great Britain by Bloomsbury Publishing Plc

First U.S. Edition: March 2010

10 9 8 7 6 5 4 3 2

# A DEDICATION

To our parents, who must be so proud.

# AN INTRODUCTION
# THIS MUCH WE KNOW

We live in a beautiful, enchanting world, a startling universe resplendent with a cornucopia of multitudinous delights – the laughter of a child; the first rainfall after an endless, sweltering summer; the twinkling reflection of a full moon over a calm midnight lake on a cool autumnal night; a freshly baked ciabatta, straight from a Tuscan oven, bristling with peppery salami and just-ripened avocado, coquettishly handed to you by an olive-skinned, raven-haired, nubile signorina.

This much we know.

Oh yeah, and there are some things that look like c**ks.

# A DISCLAIMER

BEN AND JACK THINK IT IS IMPORTANT
IMAGES CONTAINED WITHIN THIS BOOK
NOT FIDDLED WITH IN ANY WAY.

HAT YOU KNOW THAT ALL OF THE
RE UNMOLESTED, UNTOUCHED AND

THEY ARE AS NATURE INTENDED.

# HOLE-IN-ONE (TESTICLE)

## PROS

Tee off from the helmet, whack off the shaft, tickle off the scrote, and tease gently into the hole. Amigos, that's minigolf.

## CONS

The flagpole?

**34% C\*\*K**

A GOOD WALK SOILED

# MOST LIKELY TO SUCCEED

## PROS
Awesome, all the way from its stylish Mohican down to its rosy red radishes. This pampered pretty boy is really gonna break some hearts. Lucky prick.

## CONS
Sadly, his nuts have defected to the dark side. Although, one has to admit, that's a fantastic set of nips.

**82% C\*\*K**
THE BEST A MAN CAN GET

# VATICAN DECLARE 'MYSTERY ILLNESS' AS REASONS FOR POPE NO SHOW AT HISTORIC ADDRESS

## PROS

But your Holiness, there are 400,000
people out there awaiting your speech.
And honestly, I really like the new balcony.
From the front it looks much more like
St Peter cradling two watermelons.

## CONS

Watermelons?! Waterf**kingmelons!!
We both know what it looks like, and there's
no way I'm speaking about the merits of
contraception flanked by a couple of wangers.
The rubbers stay off!

**52% C\*\*K**
**GOD MOVES IN MYSTERIOUS WAYS**

# H₂OHHHHHHH

## PROS

Extreme rigidity with real potential
for growth. So rare these days to come
across a proper stonk on in the field.
Simply marvelous.

## CONS

Bizarre, feathery cockring, hopeless
ballage which defies cataloguing.
Utter chaos.

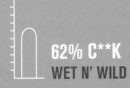

**62% C\*\*K**
WET N' WILD

# FIRST COME,
# FIRST SERVED

## PROS

For starters I'll have the balled melon,
and for mains I'll have Chef's spicy
sausage with his creamy mash potatoes
and a side of tossed salad. And can you
slap some of that hot mustard on me?

## CONS

Very good, Sir. And for dessert,
I can heartily recommend the cheese.
It's very, very smelly.

**42% C\*\*K**
**WHAT TIME DO YOU GET OFF?**

# APOLLO 69?

## PROS
Built by stoned NASA engineers in 1971 for a mission to probe the nether regions of Uranus and the fabled brown ring of Saturn, before dropping its fat load over Venus.

## CONS
Sadly the project never got to first base and was canned once President Nixon got wind of it and told everyone at NASA to lay the hell off them doobies.

**42% C**K**
IN SPACE, NO ONE CAN HEAR YOU CREAM

# COME FRIENDLY DONGS AND FALL ON SLOUGH

## PROS
Graceful, craning arc and inquisitive posture suggest questing personality and good sense of humor.

## CONS
It's half a mile away!

**48% C\*\*K**
PULL OFF AT THE NEXT JUNCTION

# LAZY LOB IN THE ARIZONA DESERT

## PROS
Impressive rigidity. Inspiring angle which reminds one of semi-arousal of supine male.

## CONS
Hypertrophic, shaved ballage which no one likes.

**86% C\*\*K**
**A ROCK AND A HARD PLACE**

# MARAUDING SKY-DONGER

## PROS
Heroic representation. Well-defined
helmet and appropriate shading.

## CONS
Heavily distended urethra suggests
botched circumcision as teenager.

**94% C\*\*K**
IT CAME FROM ABOVE

# BAFFLED POLICE SEARCH FOR LEADS AS VIAGRA MUGGERS STRIKE AGAIN

## PROS

I never saw it coming. One minute I was walking home through the forest, the next minute I came to with a pounding headache, leaves in my hair, and a dirty great tear in the front of my pants.

## CONS

Stop staring Detective Kowalski! Can't you see the man's been through enough?

**93% C\*\*K**
C\*\*KS AND ROBBERS

# A C\*\*K IS FOR LIFE,
# NOT JUST FOR CHRISTMAS

## PROS

We found poor Tito after a call from a concerned neighbor alerted us to his dreadful plight. We don't normally take in cactuses here at the sanctuary, but Tito was a special case and the other puppies took to him very quickly.

## CONS

A fresh bowl of chow and a good tummy rub would normally get them out into the yard, but so far Tito has failed to respond; although his balls seem to like it.

### 64% C\*\*K

FOR JUST $5 A MONTH, YOU CAN STOP US TYING TITO TO A BRICK AND LOBBING HIM INTO THE CANAL

# MAN CAUGHT IN IMPOSSIBLE FELLATIO SCENARIO

## PROS
Rare sighting of beautifully proportioned albino thumper. And, for the love of God, he's kissing it!

## CONS
Abortive Prince Albert piercing hole and terrifying helmet scars.

 **53% C\*\*K**
**HE'S GONNA BLOW!**

# CAPE COD SUMMER FAIR RUINED BY LATE ENTRY

## PROS

Punishing girth, walloping great ballbags, preposterous length, vestigial foreskin doubling as handle... Wow! Oh, and at just under 3ft, this delightful specimen can still be loaded as hand-luggage.

## CONS

Precious few to mention. One of those rare, happy instances where criticism would be churlish, like chastising the gardener for growing inappropriate vegetables.

**82% C\*\*K**
**FOR CHRISSAKES DOROTHY, GET YOUR COAT, WE'RE LEAVING**

# YOU SAY TOMATO, I SAY C**K

## PROS
Enthusiastic pubic growth. Lovely, polished, glossy willy. Edible penis always a bonus.

## CONS
Complete absence of man cherries and faint air of femininity may point to this not being a c**k at all. Overgrown clitoris; run for the hills!

**60% C**K**
LET'S CALL THE WHOLE THING A BIG UGLY
C**K TOMATO WITH A SCREWY STALK

# REARGUARD ACTION BREAKTHROUGH FOR CRACK GERMAN SAUSAGE DIVISION

## PROS

For a conventionally solitary, unruly beast, such strength in numbers is a rare and exciting find. Their leader has disciplined his boys well.

## CONS

It's as we always feared – the Hun cloned the c**k!

**61% C**K**
YAR, YAR, PIETER, DAS EINE GROSSEN SAUSAGEHAUSER!

# STUNNED PALAEONTOLOGISTS UNEARTH CATEGORICAL EVIDENCE OF THE FABLED C\*\*KOSAURUS

## PROS

100% anatomically correct, with
inch-perfect ratio of girth to length,
accompanied by a lovely big set of nuts
that really frame this enchanting scene.
And to cap it all, it's a beautiful
day for a bike ride.

## CONS

The team broke a lot of spades in the rush
to reveal this prehistoric marvel. And the
poor saps are still digging for the helmet.

**79% C\*\*K**
JURASSIC PORK

# WELCOME TO LONDON'S C**KLANDS

## PROS

Perfect c**kage with self-cleansing nob end courtesy of Old Father Thames.

## CONS

A little on the short side. On the soft? Dresses to the left – hopelessly out of fashion!

**49% C**K**
**DODGY C**KNEY**

# ICE GUYS FINISH LAST

## PROS

GRETZKY LOOKS TO SCORE: Soft, free-thinking, artistic, with GSOH. Loves animals, long walks, ice-skating. WLTM female with cold hands. What's wrong with just being a really nice guy?

## CONS

Hi, it's me. I know we had a great time last night at the rink, but I've realized that I see you more as a friend than anything else. And seriously, this has absolutely nothing to do with your total lack of chestnuts. ☹

**31% C\*\*K**
**IT'S OKAY, WE CAN JUST HOLD HANDS**

# WHAT DO YOU CALL A MAN WITH A 200FT STONE PENIS?

## PROS

No pant could ever claim to tame this monstrous Frankenc**k (although to be fair, none have tried). Erosion has done for the minor body parts, but 'Big Tufty' just won't go down.

## CONS

Semi-derelict state has left Big Tufty all alone, save for his patchy and unsettling pubic growth. 'Why you laugh at Big Tufty? Big Tufty have feelings too.'

**57% C**K**
PAY ATTENTION, HE'S CALLED BIG TUFTY

# ROBOC\*\*K

## PROS

Too quick with the zipper? Shut yourself in
the shower door? Hang-glided into a cactus?
Your prayers are answered! New Roboc\*\*k
3000 comes equipped with solid steel
thunder stick, 3-speed auto-thruster and
revolutionary jet-powered Detachoballs™. †

## CONS

† Roboc\*\*k Ltd accepts absolutely no
responsibility for spontaneous take-off
of Detachoballs™.

**22% C\*\*K**
**READ INSTRUCTIONS**
**CAREFULLY BEFORE USE**

# IF YOU GO DOWN TO THE WOODS TODAY…

## PROS

Cleft helmet a real life-saver for those hot, sticky summers, topped off with some excellent filigree work that exhibits a naughty sense of the absurd.

## CONS

Just like Mama's chili con carne, smooth as silk on the way in, rough as old boots on the way out.

81% C**K
CAN'T SEE THE TREES FOR THE WOOD

# GARDENER SUSPENDED OVER INSENSITIVE PLANTING FOR WHITE HOUSE SUMMER PARTY

## PROS

Placed in convivial surroundings and given time to mature, this cross-gartered, multi-balled exotic makes for a lovely conversation piece. Shame, Monica would have loved it…

## CONS

The party was grooving until that asshole Rahm Emanuel gave it a tickle and all hell broke loose. The puppies shat up the new basketball courts, Hilary chinned Barack and Michelle's holed herself up in the Oval Office.

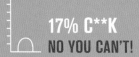

**17% C\*\*K**
**NO YOU CAN'T!**

# FROZEN JEWISH PECKER RIDES THE SEVEN SEAS

## PROS
Crisp, deep and even sculpture of classic communal shower c**k (turn 90 degrees). Gives global warming a good name.

## CONS
Unnerving combination of young man's 'head' on old man's 'shoulders'.

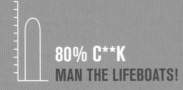

**80% C**K**
**MAN THE LIFEBOATS!**

# DR PENISTONE, I PRESUME

## PROS

Day 27: Dearest Jenkins, I write to you in a state of extreme arousal. We came across the mighty Wang-Tu-Tu this morning, mercifully sleeping off the exertions of the night before. The wager is won, the museum is saved and you might want to put down fresh sawdust in the guest bedroom.

## CONS

Such was the ferocity of the encounter that my hitherto trusted companion Matubu turned heel and legged it into the scrub, taking with him my good trousers, an ounce of raspberry tobacco and what was left of the Grey Poupon.

**76% C**K**
CAGING THE BEAST

# JOHNSON 3:16

## PROS

For God so loved the world that He thrust
upon us His terrifying tumescence so we
might feel humbled and insecure every time
we drop our Y-fronts.

## CONS

And lo, on the fourth day God regretted
His childish prank, and there was very
little rejoicing.

**8% C\*\*K**
ALL HAIL THE SECOND COMING

# FEMALE GOLF PROFESSIONAL CELEBRATES LATEST VICTORY AND TAKES HOME YETI'S MEAT

## PROS

Delicate, reverential handling exhibits rightful respect for this frankly awesome locker room favorite.

## CONS

Rectangular scrotum, dimpled bell-end, overly planed shaft – home DIY enthusiast?

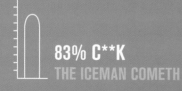

**83% C\*\*K**
THE ICEMAN COMETH

# JUST WHEN YOU THOUGHT IT WAS SAFE TO GO BACK IN THE WATER

## PROS

'Understand this, Chief. I'm the Mayor of this town and you must be one clam short of a Vongole if you think I'm going to close down the beaches because you've seen another man-eater in the water.'

## CONS

'Don't you see? This ain't no kissy-girl dolphin, this ain't no faggoty shark, this is a c**k, goddammit! Have you seen what these things can do to people? Now, I'm gonna need a fishing rod, a pair of thigh-high waders, and a laminated picture of your wife.'

**45% C**K**
**THAT WAS NO BOAT ACCIDENT**

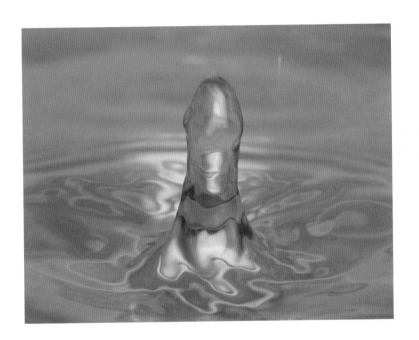

# FOOTBALL TEAM ILL AT EASE WITH REFEREE'S UNORTHODOX APPROACH TO PRE-MATCH STUD INSPECTION

## PROS

Game-winning thunder thighs leading up to a streamlined set of buns so tight you could bounce a silver dollar off them.

## CONS

Hairy ass crack a definite hazard in the line of scrimmage. Unnecessary roughness: 15 yard penalty.

73% C**K

HE... COULD... GO... ALL... THE... WAY!

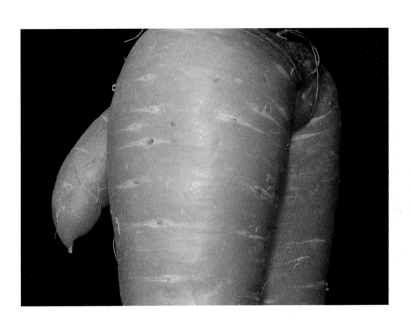

# GOODNESS, GRACIOUS, GREAT BALLS OF FIRE

## PROS

Crimson red, unspoiled, virginal package,
just ripe for the picking. Dimpled surface
area will control overheating and prevent
the torture of sweaty ballbags
(and associated chafing).

## CONS

The splendor of this guy's mighty stones
suggest that he's been waiting patiently for
Ms Right. CODE RED! The next girl to turn
on this tiny tap better have her skirt tucked
into her knickers.

**61% C\*\*K**
**POPPING THE CHERRY**

# OUT AND ABOUT WITH GORDON GEKKO'S WANG

## PROS

A handsome, gregarious go-getter.
Top-of-the-range executive penis
to subdue ambitious underlings and
boardroom flare-ups.

## CONS

Completely inconsiderate and highly
impractical. For business use only.

**73% C\*\*K**
REAL MEN DON'T EAT QUICHE

# WIDOW DISTRAUGHT AS HUSBAND'S WAKE IS EMPTIED BY SON-IN-LAW'S TASTELESS OFFERING

## PROS

Hi. Can I order a floral tribute, mainly blue and white flowers? I don't know, say seventy roses with a bit of foliage. Oh, and, can you make it in the shape of a c**k, please?

## CONS

Not good enough for your daughter, was I? Hope you like the flowers, you old dead bastard.

**65% C**K**
**IS NOTHING SACRED?**

# GEORGE HARRISON'S LOVE WAND HEADLINES BEATLES MEMORABILIA AUCTION

## PROS

A unique chance to own this very special portion of the Fab Four. Practically in mint condition, George's infamous chopper was reputedly inspiration for such memorable hits as 'Come Together', 'Don't Let Me Down', 'The Long and Winding Road', 'You've Got to Hide Your Love' and 'Norwegian Wood'.

## CONS

Sadly, the certificate of authenticity was misplaced in transit, but Ringo says that this is definitely George's rhythm stick.

**37% C**K**
ALL YOU NEED IS LOVE

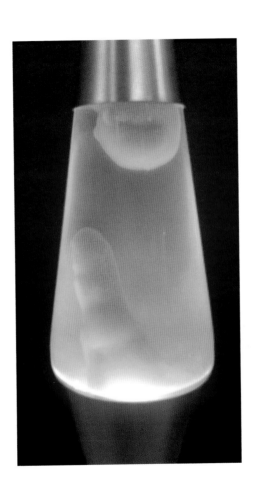

# PORKY'S APPRECIATION SOCIETY BANNED BY HARVARD AFTER DEAN'S OFFICE 'DONGED'

## PROS

Look guys, I'm a big fan of the movie too, and don't think I can't appreciate the ingenuity that went into turning my best Egyptian cotton sheets into that handsome window wanger. And, by the way, the venting in the helmet? Inspired.

## CONS

But after you guys concealed yourselves in the cavity wall of the ladies' bathroom AND rigged up my wife's dressing room with a live webcam, I'm afraid you've taken the decision out of my hands. You brought it on yourselves boys – the PAS has shot its last bolt.

**34% C\*\*K**
MAGNA CUM LAUDE

# FIELD OF DREAMS

## PROS
Gargantuan proportions make this
the perfect pilgrimage site for all
lovers of the blue-veined flute.

## CONS
Being only visible from the air makes
this Jolly Green Giant the preserve
of the privileged few.

**69% C\*\*K**
IF YOU MOW IT, IT WILL COME

# STREET SWEEPERS WALK OUT AFTER SEWAGE WORKERS' PRACTICAL JOKE TAKES A NASTY TURN

## PROS

'Come on lads, where's your sense of humor? It's only a little one. You're lucky we didn't send the balls up.'

## CONS

'It's a hard enough job at the best of times without steel penises coming at you at 100 miles an hour. That last one those idiots fired up split my broom and nearly knocked my garbage can over.'

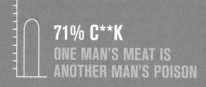

**71% C**K**
ONE MAN'S MEAT IS
ANOTHER MAN'S POISON

# THE BIGGER THEY COME, THE HARDER THEY FALL

## PROS

Come on big fella, don't let them see you like this. Of course they're gonna say nasty things, they're jealous. Remember what they always say, 'It's nice to put on Speedos when you're hung like a torpedo.'

## CONS

Jesus, if this is what you're like when you're sad, I'd hate to see you when you're happy. And don't think you're getting a hug either.

## 64% C**K
### DON'T BEAT YOURSELF OFF OVER IT

# NEW BRANCH OF CONTROVERSIAL CHURCH OF C**KOLOGY OFF TO SLOW START

## PROS

Founded upon the teachings of Bhagwan Shree Tom Selleck, C**kology preaches the compulsory wearing of short terry cloth dressing-gowns, the euphoria of high-waisted tight jeans and some other weird stuff about aliens and chest wigs and arousing topiary.

## CONS

We've been open for 3 weeks and all we've got is Shaggy and Scooby sitting out there stoned in the hippie wagon. Better call Selleck's brother and tell him the talk's off.

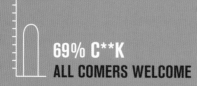

**69% C**K**
**ALL COMERS WELCOME**

# YOUNG BRIDE SUMMONS EXORCIST AS X-RATED HAUNTING CONTINUES

## PROS

Father, it happened again last night, exactly like before. Soon after my husband came to bed, I heard the toilet flush, there was a rustling under the covers, followed by a loud groan, then a big, hot wad of something hit me in the face.

## CONS

Hush my child, everything will be fine. Sexorcisms like this are simple affairs: pop a bottle of wine in the ice box, put on some Enya, run a hot, soapy bath, and I'll slip on a cassock and my best crucifix and be at yours in half an hour.

**20% C\*\*K**
**IT CAME FROM BEYOND**

# IS IT A BIRD, IS IT A PLANE...?

## PROS

By day a mild-mannered, cheese-shaped office building, by night a 400ft crime-fighting brick dick.

## CONS

Massive concrete foundations and underground car park mean that unless the crime occurs within the immediate vicinity, this frustrated daredevil is of absolutely no use.

48% C\*\*K
NO, IT'S CAPTAIN STIFFY!

# ANIMAL, VEGETABLE, MINERAL...
# PENIS?

## PROS

Stuffed with sausage and topped with a melted Dutch
gouda, this hot and handsome devil makes
for an electric accompaniment to a pigeon breast
and cous cous main. Bon appetit!

## CONS

Whoa there big fella, this dirty beast is for dinner with
your mistress, not supper with the wife. Remember,
it's your children she's kissing with that mouth.

**62% C\*\*K**
TASTE THE DIFFERENCE

# UNUSUAL NEW VENDING MACHINE A SURPRISE SENSATION IN DOWNTOWN DALLAS

## PROS

The Derringer – Great for sports and tight, tight shorts: $50

Colt 45 – Versatile yet with imposing heft. Although mostly a social penis, this sharpshooter won't let you down between the sheets: $100

44 Magnum – It'll blow your head clean off!: $200

## CONS

Customers are advised not to drink, drive or operate heavy machinery while wielding the 44 Magnum.

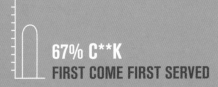

**67% C\*\*K**
**FIRST COME FIRST SERVED**

# MAVERICK CEO STANDS ALONE IN DEBATE ON THE MOTIVATIONAL POWERS OF HAVING A GREAT BIG C**K IN THE LOBBY

## PROS

Machine-cut scrotum ensures perfectly rounded, revolving ballage and provides an ideal launchpad for ergonomically designed shaft, which will heighten productivity whilst reducing operator fatigue and discomfort, which is nice.

## CONS

Stair access to 'Biffin's Bridge' is useful for inspection and storage etc. But in practice the whole endeavor is a flaming assault on decency and smacks of corporate arrogance on a grand scale. Blue sky thinking my ass.

## 42% C**K

REMEMBER GUYS, PEOPLE LAUGHED AT CHRIS COLUMBUS WHEN HE SAID 'I'M OFF TO AMERICA'. WHO'S LAUGHING NOW?

# MIRROR, MIRROR ON THE WALL, WHO'S GOT THE BIGGEST WANGER OF ALL?

## PROS

The other dwarfs never believed Snow White when she said there was something special about Dopey, until that morning in the showers.

## CONS

Bad news – size does matter.

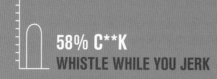

**58% C\*\*K**
WHISTLE WHILE YOU JERK

# I WANDERED SEXY AS A CLOUD

## PROS

Ladies, I can tell you lookin' and I know you
like what you see. And I know what you
askin' yourselves and the answer is yes –
I'm all natural. Now charter a goddamn 747
and get your asses up here.

## CONS

It gets so lonely up here, the only ladies
I meet are air hostesses, and don't think
I can't hear them screamin' through them
Pyrex windows.

**78% C\*\*K**
**BABY, IT'S MY DUTY, AND I'M ALWAYS FREE**

# CALIFORNIA-BASED IMPOTENCY CLINIC UNVEILS CONTROVERSIAL NEW 'C**K GARDEN'

## PROS

Here at the Ironman Clinic, we're all about personal growth. Our guests kick off the morning with a stimulating breakfast of 20 oysters and 3 pints of Guinness. Then it's straight into our private movie theater for a 3 hour European pornfest. After a light snack lunch, the highlight of the day comes with a stirring 5 hour rock-hugging session in the garden.

## CONS

Nurse was positive she saw an erection last week, but unfortunately she also had to deal with 5 cases of extreme heat exhaustion and 27 cases of food poisoning. As of next week we'll be changing our caterers.

**54% C**K**
**REACH FOR THE SKIES**

# EARLY PROTOTYPE FOR ABANDONED WAR C**K

## PROS

Phenomenal bell-end, gratifyingly disproportionate to lean shaft and surrounding vegetation. Cunningly placed release valve to alleviate symptoms of blue balls.

## CONS

A showpiece c**k, which requires military clearance and small crane for use.

**76% C**K**

MAKE LOVE NOT WAR

# F**K NOSE WHAT'S GOING ON HERE

## PROS

What you see is what you get.
This lucky dude wears his heart on
his sleeve and his c**k on his face.
Ladies, form an orderly line.

## CONS

Undescended left bollock could lead to
complications in later life. Caution! When
erect, subject's vision is totally obscured.

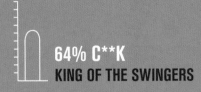

**64% C**K**
**KING OF THE SWINGERS**

# WHO PUT THIS ONE IN HERE?

## PROS
It looks quite bendy. Is that good?

## CONS
Ah man, there's just so much wrong with it.
It's got little legs, some weird rocky thing
where its pubes should be and it moves so
slowly it's gonna be around for ages. And
why is it so wet…?

## 0% C**K
WELL, THAT JUST ABOUT
RUINS THE WHOLE BOOK

# PICTURE ACKNOWLEDGMENTS

Ben and Jack would like to thank the following for providing photographs. While every effort has been made to trace and acknowledge all copyright holders, we would like to apologize should there have been any errors or omissions, unless you're that asshole who didn't get back to us after we emailed you 15 times.

**Ice Guys Finish Last** – Jonathan Bein
**Lazy Lob** – dpd photo
(www.flickr.com/photos/dpdphoto)
**200ft Penis** – Juho Vähä-Herttua
**Marauding Sky Donger** – Jodie Hunter
**Field of Dreams** – Duncan Brooks
**You Say Tomato** – Paul Fontana
**A C\*\*k is For Life** – Jay Freeman
**German Sausage Division** – Christiane Moore
(www.christiane.paperpetual.com)
**Mirror, Mirror On the Wall** – Traci Clevenger
**Balls of Fire** – Mireille Sillander
**Johnson 3:16** – Henry M K Diaz
**Just When You Thought It Was Safe** – Matthieu Collomp
**Who Put This One in Here?** – Amanda Sipa
**Most Likely To Succeed** – Bob Cafarelli
**Apollo 69?** – J P Schneider

Roboc\*\*k – Keith Meng-wei Loh
Sexy As a Cloud – James Dobson
George Harrison's Love Wand – Jim
The Harder They Come – Josh Homme
Street Sweepers – Gabi Helfert
Gardener Suspended – Christina Pedersen
Animal, Vegetable, Mineral – James Broad
(www.flickr.com/photos/kulor)
Church of C\*\*kology – Stacy Cochrell
Slough – Jack (Ben driving)
Cape Cod Summer Fair – Graham Samuel
Frozen Jewish Pecker – Rex Features
Impossible Fellatio Scenario – Corbis
C\*\*klands – Courtesy of the TopSat consortium © QinetiQ
F\*\*k Nose – Corbis
Female Golf Pro – Empics
Football Team III At Ease – Rex Features
Dr Penistone – Jason J. Corneveaux
Is It a Bird – Marina Silva
Distraught Widow – Laura Riseam
Maverick CEO – Ben
(Jack holding legs and Shane Allen spotting)
First Come, First Served – Dan Franklin
H$_2$OHHHHHHH – Rick Davy
Vatican Declare Mystery Illness – Clement Biger
Hole-In-One – Jase Wells (www.flickr.com/photos/sfjase/2880590567/)

# ACKNOWLEDGMENTS

Ben and Jack would like to thank:
Antony Topping; Daniel Greenberg; Richard Atkinson and all at Bloomsbury; Marc Resnick and all at St. Martin's Press; the design genius of Unreal; Richard Bravery; Michelle Kane; Jamie H-W; Jess, Ellie and Theo; Chairman, Chairwoman, Ben and Anna; and, of course, Simon Collins for his monkey magic.